TO BUILD A SUSTAINABLE LEGACY

100 Lessons

to

Equip Family Leaders
to Preserve the Family
and its Wealth

Tom Fowler

Six-Word Lessons to Build a Sustainable Legacy – 6wordlessons.com

Copyright ©2010 by Tom Fowler

Published by Leading on the Edge International
704 228th Avenue NE #703
Sammamish WA 98074
leadingonedge.com

ISBN-10: 1-933750-28-6
ISBN-13: 978-1-933750-28-6

Part of the lore surrounding the writer, Ernest Hemingway is a bet he made that he could write a complete story using just six words. He won the bet. His story was, "For sale, baby shoes, never worn." Even though there were just six words, the mind supplies the details.

Exploring the story further, I found there is a vast universe of people and organizations who continue to pursue Hemingway's six word challenge. Enter "six word stories" into your internet search engine and this universe will open to you.

Over coffee one morning, I shared the Hemingway story with Lonnie Pacelli, a friend with an inquisitive and creative mind. Lonnie is a prolific author, a successful business owner, and a management consultant. He seized the idea of creating a series of books based on the six word concept. He wrote his first book in a matter of weeks and challenged me to create my own six word concept book. It is his brain child that led me to write *Six Word Lessons to Build a Sustainable Legacy*.

Prologue

The concepts in this book come from my forty plus years of experience working with family owned businesses. I have seen families who were very successful in creating and sustaining their family legacies. I have also seen too many families who self-destructed because of numerous problems stemming from lack of communication, dysfunctional relationships, and a lack of positive mentoring of future generations. Although money does exacerbate the problem, families often fail to stay together through multiple generations regardless of whatever wealth is involved.

The inability to successfully keep the family and the family wealth together through multiple generations is centuries old and international in scope. There is a familiar quote dating back to the Ming Dynasty: "Fu bu guo san dai" or, "Wealth does not pass three generations." This is because the second generation may see the value of the hard work that achieved the wealth, but the third generation won't. History also tells of great kings who made tremendous contributions to their empires, only to have sons destroy all their accomplishments in a matter of years. Solomon, the richest and most successful king in ancient history had a son, Rehoboam, whose mismanagement of the kingdom led to a people's revolt. How did this happen to the son of the wisest man in history? Rehoboam rejected the counsel of his father's advisors in favor of the advice of his peers. After your death, one of the first decisions your children will make is the choice of an advisor. How will they make the best choice if they have not been mentored by you?

In my travels, I have had the opportunity to talk with people from various parts of the world. Their stories and concerns for their family legacies are universal. I visited a family in Finland. The visit included a tour of the family home and farm. I asked the oldest child how the decision was made as to who would live in the house after the parents were gone (the one who lived in the ancestral home was considered the family leader). She said, "Very poorly." The family included several children and their spouses. Communication between the parents and the children was nonexistent as it related to the family inheritance. Decisions regarding family wealth were being made in a vacuum. The lack of communication between the parents and the children was creating family dissention. Similar stories exist in all cultures.

Inheritance and wealth are often regarded as taboo subjects by parents. Children are reluctant to approach their parents to discuss planning because they don't want to appear greedy. Parents, who consider they have a close relationship with their children, overlook the impact their wealth will have on their grandchildren. By the time their children receive their inheritance, their lifestyle will be set. The grandchildren may not be prepared to handle a financial inheritance. Who will mentor the grandchildren if you do not create a method of communication and training that lasts through generations? Thus, the question remains, how can I keep my family and the family wealth together through subsequent generations?

To answer this question for myself and ultimately for my clients, I started researching the concept of legacy planning. A legacy is defined as "a gift of property or anything handed down from the past." The legacy we hand down to future generations is more than wealth. It also includes values, vision, and goals. It is the instructions we prepare for a generation we will not see.

I joined professional organizations, pursued continuing education, and read volumes of books and other literature. The one thing lacking was the process that passed the values with the wealth. This was true until I joined The Heritage Institute (THI) as a charter member. THI was founded by Perry Cochell and Rod Zeeb. THI came from their joint experience that traditional estate planning prepared the wealth for the family but failed to prepare the family for the wealth. The purpose of THI is to educate and train professionals to assist families in keeping the wealth and the family together through multiple generations. Amazingly, only ten percent of families are able to accomplish this objective.

My experiences working with families mirror those of the founders of THI. Just like inherited wealth, family businesses rarely survive through the third generation. My approach with my clients, my thought process and my vocabulary have been influenced by my study and affiliation with THI. I have adopted their terminology and their unique process because I believe it prepares families to build sustainable legacies through subsequent generations.

My hope is that this book inspires you to launch your own legacy planning by opening your mind to ideas you had not previously considered. My work in this important area is—in many ways—the lasting legacy I contribute to others through a lifetime of study, commitment, and service. It's my honor to share essential lessons to guide you in creating your sustainable family legacy. I wish you the best in creating your family legacy.

Tom Fowler

Acknowledgments

This book is the result of a collaboration effort of many people. My special thanks go to Rod Zeeb and Perry Cochell for creating The Heritage Process, and to Carol Wheeler, Deborah Roberts and Julie Fowler who worked tirelessly editing and critiquing the manuscript. Nancy Juetten supplied the finishing touches to make this book complete.

I thank the following for their good counsel: Ryan Zeeb, Brian Bell, Bill Hughes, William Eck, Greg Bodine, Lonnie Pacelli, Brian Walters, and Steve Beals.

The test of this manuscript was the critique and insight offered by my own family. My wife, Elaine, gave me insight to clarify concepts. My children, Scott Fowler, Jennifer Savage, and Julie Fowler gave their perspectives on critical points. I am grateful for their encouragement and support in making this book a reality.

Disclosures

Tom Fowler is providing this book for client educational purposes only and is not intended to provide specific advice or recommendations for any individual situation or security product. The information being provided is strictly as a courtesy and is deemed to be reliable; however, Woodbury Financial Services makes no representation as to the completeness or accuracy of information provided. Woodbury Financial Services has not contributed to its content nor are the opinions of the authors the opinions of Woodbury. Accordingly, Woodbury Financial Services shall not be held liable for any loss or damage caused or alleged to have been caused by the use of or reliance upon the information contained herein.

Securities and Investment Advisory Services offered through Woodbury Financial Services, Inc., Member FINRA, SIPC and Registered Investment Advisor. PO Box 64284, St Paul, MN 55164. (800)800-2638. The Fowler Group and Woodbury Financial Services, Inc are not affiliated entities.

The Heritage Process is copyrighted material of The Heritage Institute (THI). Permission to copy is cheerfully granted solely to Thomas E. Fowler. Professional advisors must contact Rod Zeeb regarding a license to copy or use any THI material or concepts identified in this book.

Table of Contents

Six-Word Lessons to Build a Sustainable Legacy

Give Your History to Your Family

1

Your story is personal and unique.

Your life is a story composed of many chapters. Who you are today as a person was forged by those experiences. The stories and experiences hold the keys to your value structure. They are the basis of your true wealth.

2

Your story has value. Tell it!

Sharing your life experiences mentors future generations within your own family as well as others. Your triumphs, failures and humorous encounters illustrate important lessons others can use to navigate their way through the adventures of their own life.

3

Few children know their parents' stories.

Children have a tendency to see you as you are now. They know little of the trials, tribulations, and triumphs that got you where you are today. When you die, your stories are lost forever unless you preserve them.

4

Grandchildren are your story's greatest beneficiaries.

Your stories and the value of your experiences are your grandchildren's most valuable inheritance. Your experiences are a bridge to the past and a map to the future. If you don't tell them the stories, who will?

5

Your greatest personal failures teach volumes.

The ability to persevere through trials produces character and self confidence. Trials are often the foundation of the success one has today. The knowledge gained in these trials is what parents wish they could give their children.

6

Shared family experiences create lifetime memories.

Picture a happy family gathering, for example at a wedding or graduation. See the people. Listen to the conversations. Feel the love among the extended family. These experiences become part of the family story. The stories are the glue that bond family generations together.

7

Children/ grandchildren love hearing your stories.

A shared experience of your life allows your children and grandchildren to see you as "a real person" with whom they can identify. Your stories open avenues of communication and enhanced relationships.

8

Children/ grandchildren love hearing their stories.

Children often ask, "Tell me a story of when I was little." They want to know they had a place and a value in the family and memories of them are precious to you. Never miss an opportunity to share those memories.

9

Preserve your story. Keep a journal.

A man once told me he met his father through his father's journals. Were it not for personal journals, much of our history would be lost. Preserve your story, keep a journal. The best thing about writing a journal is that it allows you to measure your progress through life.

10

Your story is your personal immortality.

Families who stay together through multiple generations know their family story. They value the rich traditions of the family experiences which bond them together. You will be remembered through your story, but only if you are intentional in preserving it.

Define Your Values, Build Upon Them

11

Most people cannot articulate their values.

Everyone has a code of values. Most people can't articulate the basis for their moral code. To create a sustainable legacy you have to be able to communicate why an individual value is important to you, otherwise; it loses significance for the next generation.

12

Personal reflection reveals your true values.

Have you ever dedicated time to reflect on the significant events that shaped your world view? These are the foundations for the values you learned from your life's experiences. They are seldom defined by tangible wealth.

13

Consider your mentors, they reveal values.

Consider those people who made a positive impact on your life like a parent, teacher, or coach. The traits you admired in them are the values you esteem. They are also the values you already possess.

14

Your associates reflect your character values.

Examine your closest associates. What is it that attracts you to them? A close inspection reveals they share your common values. This is an important lesson to share with your children and grandchildren. You will be known by those with whom you associate.

15

Mentor children/ grandchildren in your values.

What additional values should you share with your children and grandchildren that you have not yet communicated? Why are they important? Explain how your life's experiences impacted you to cement those values in your life.

16

Values determine your course of action.

Your values create the blueprint for your actions. What material wealth you leave your children, how you spend your material and social capital, and the organizations you support are all determined by your values. Your values are why you do what you do.

17

Communicate your values to your beneficiaries.

It makes sense to communicate your values to the beneficiaries of your bounty. If you leave assets to a charity, they should know why you chose them and how they fit with your personal values. The same is true for family.

18

Your legacy is defined by values.

Your story is defined by the values you demonstrated in life. Eulogies are not focused on accomplishments. They are celebrations of the contributions you made to the lives of others. Create the legacy you desire.

19

Family values are the true inheritance.

When one thinks of receiving an inheritance, they usually think of material assets. "How much do I get?" is often the question asked by heirs. They don't realize they have already received their true inheritance, the values you passed to them.

20

Families united by values survive generations.

Families who remain together through successive generations are united by family values. Their sense of purpose is defined by the family history and by the values which they hold sacred. These values are passed from generation to generation.

Define Success. What's Important to You?

21

Success isn't measured by tangible assets.

Material assets may be a good measure of how successful you are in your career but they may not be a good definition of success. Personal success is measured by the wealth of your experiences which allow you to create the life you have today.

22

Success doesn't define who you are.

Success is not defined by who you are, the title you have, or how big your balance sheet is. It is defined by where you are in life today. Define your success by the difference you make in the lives of others.

23

Define success by your personal life.

A financially wealthy individual once defined success to me as, "Having a job you love and a warm home for your family." Loving families and the concept of home are not obtained by material wealth. They are created by love.

24

Success measurements are often very small.

A young quadriplegic told me his greatest success was to be able to propel his wheelchair across the door threshold by himself. It was the beginning of his independence. The turning point in your life may be insignificant to others, but a life defining moment for you.

25

Family financial success takes intentional planning.

Wealth can open the doors to many opportunities. It can fund education. It can assist family members in starting new businesses. It can be used to advance the work of charitable causes. If wealth management is part of your definition of success, it takes intention to make it happen.

26

Help your children achieve financial success.

In many families money is a taboo subject rarely discussed. Most parents want their children to be financially stable, financially independent, debt free, and prepared for the future. Teach them the principles of financial management.

27

Family, a measurement of your success.

Some measurements of success are the qualities of respect, reverence and honesty you inspire in your children. Success is having all your children and grandchildren become responsible, respectable adults, marked by mutual honor and close relationships.

28

Write your eulogy
to evaluate success.

A eulogy is a forward looking statement that defines how you want to be remembered in life. It usually focuses on the character qualities you hope others will see and recognize in your life. Write your eulogy.

29

Generation to generation, success measurement differs.

How does your definition of success differ from your parents? How will your definition differ from your children and grand-children? They will never know what is really important to you unless you mentor them.

30

Success is defined by your values.

Your core values are reflected in how you define success. That which is important to you is part of your true inheritance and legacy that passes to the next generation. A family that stays together knows how the family success is defined and measured.

Shirtsleeves to Shirtsleeves in Three Generations

31

70% of estate plans will fail.

Proverbs dating from the Ming Dynasty to the present tell us that wealth seldom remains in the same family through three generations. Author E.G. "Jay" Link, writes that there is a seventy percent failure rate in passing wealth from one generation to the next, and ninety percent is lost by the third generation.

32

Be a Rothschild not a Vanderbilt.

The Rothschilds remain one of the most powerful and wealthy families in the world. The family and their wealth have survived numerous generations and continue to do so today. The Vanderbilts squandered their wealth and their family in three generations.

33

Intentionally prepare to beat plan failures.

Seventy percent of estate planning fails, not from poor advice, but from failure to prepare the family for the wealth. Successful wealth transfer through multiple generations takes intentional planning and execution of the plan.

34

Wealth earned. Children indulged. Generations lost.

King Solomon, the wisest and richest person who ever lived, said it is vanity of vanities for a man to accumulate great wealth and to leave it to someone who neither worked for it nor appreciates it.

35

Indulgences can start with good intentions.

How long does it take a good intention to become an indulgence in the eyes of your children and grandchildren? Exercise caution and restraint with gift giving. A luxury once lived becomes a necessity.

36

Affluenza, a dysfunctional relationship with money.

A person who loves money will not be satisfied by it. The Vanderbilts destroyed their wealth and their family with reckless consumption. They squandered an inheritance of $143 billion (in 2007 dollars) in legendary fashion. Little remained of the wealth by the end of the third generation.

37

Consider how much wealth is enough.

Warren Buffett says, "A very rich person should leave his kids enough to do anything but not enough to do nothing." Without mentoring, wealth can destroy initiative.

38

Money is a tool. Training required.

Money is a powerful tool. In the proper hands it can provide countless opportunities for good for the family and for others. Without training, its use can be destructive and debilitating to the family.

39

Good intentions can have unintended consequences.

How many people do you know whose lives have been destroyed by wealth? The best intentions can lead to incentive-killing indulgences. Teach your children and grandchildren the values that will help them become men and women of character.

40

Money mentoring starts in early childhood.

Children can learn the value of money and its use by giving them age-appropriate activities. Let them earn money by doing extra chores. Encourage savings. Guide them to learn the gift of charity by giving a token of what they've earned to others less fortunate.

Equip Family Generations for Inherited Wealth

41

Give your children a pre-inheritance experience.

Pre-inheritance experiences help to prepare children to receive both their financial inheritance (and responsibilities) and their emotional inheritance. They prepare succeeding generations for the responsibilities of life, wealth management and stewardship. They begin the transfer of leadership within the family.

42

Family governance begins the equipping process.

A structured process is necessary to keep a family and its wealth intact through subsequent generations. The process requires the family to work together as a multigenerational team to achieve goals established by the family.

43

Family governance focuses on family business.

Family governance is where the business of the family (not investments or business entities owned by the family) can be conducted for multiple generations. Family business is unique to your family. It is built upon communication, active mentoring, and encouragement of individual and collective family member achievement.

44

The family council creates multi-generational leadership.

The council is the structure created to accomplish the family's objectives. It varies from family to family. The purpose of the family council meeting is family fun, family development, and business of the family (not any family business they may own or operate).

45

Create the classroom, mentor future generations.

The family council is the children and grand-children's hands-on classroom to equip them with the skills and talents they will need for the inheritance they will receive. Through the ongoing family council, each succeeding generation is mentored and prepared by the previous generation.

46

Each participant attends for their reasons.

Each family member must decide to participate in the family council for his or her own reasons. It will be worth attending if the governance structure provides that each voice will be heard and each individual finds a productive outlet for his or her core passions.

47

The family council is the family.

Those who attend the family council can be the entire family: children, in-laws, grand-children, and beyond. Everyone's participation is encouraged, recognizing that each family is unique. In reality, the family will invite the participation of everyone with whom they are comfortable.

48

Focus on hands-on learning, not results.

Initially, parents' expectations are often on results rather than hands-on learning. Effective family governance should focus first on creating and managing structures that give the heirs information, education, and real world training.

49

Preparing parents/ leaders essential for success.

Preparing parents in the governance experience is important. If parents focus on results rather than lessons learned, strong personalities will dominate the meetings. The desired outcome is making sure every family member understands that their voice and their participation have equal value.

50

Passing life experiences, a fundamental objective.

Part of the pre-inheritance experience is passing family stories, life lessons, values, methods, standards and principles to the next generation. This is fundamental to the object of preparing the next generation for the emotional and the financial inheritance they will receive.

Understanding Family Roles Creates Lasting Legacies

51

The family organization defines family actions.

The family is the basic organizational unit. It establishes the "operations manual" which defines who we are, how we view the world, and how we make decisions. It defines behavior. It can be fragmented and dysfunctional or united in purpose and vision.

52

The family structure defines individual roles.

A family contains many roles: mom, dad, son, daughter, in-law, spouse, grandchild, etc. An individual defined by role often feels powerless, blames others, and creates tension. When you are walking on egg shells, you are reacting from position. Look beyond your position and see the whole.

53

Your role doesn't define your contribution.

Your value and contribution to the family are not limited to the boundaries of your role. Healthy families recognize and acknowledge the value and the unique talents each person contributes to the family. This is essential to building a sustainable legacy.

54

Know your role before you speak.

When you interact in family discussions, determine which role you are in before you speak. Look beyond position so you can make a decision or contribution from the right perspective.

55

The leader's role: transition is inevitable.

A change in leadership is never an "if." It is a certainty. What you do today will determine how well prepared your family will be to manage the transition and to keep the family and its wealth intact through multiple generations.

56

Monarch to mentor: the legacy transition.

Many families are dominated from the top down. The family leader (Monarch) rules with an iron fist until he or she is forced out by death or revolt. Mentors plan their departures by passing the mantle of leadership to the next generation.

57

Facilitating the transfer: leader to mentor.

Implementing the legacy process is a transitional event. Passing the leadership role from the current family head to the next generation of family leadership is the transition from leader to mentor. How you handle it will determine future family relationships.

58

The ultimate role: the intergenerational mentor.

The mentor prepares the family to assume responsibility for intentional, intergenerational leadership. Mentorship requires patience, encouragement, and constructive criticism. It requires the ablility to recognize and nurture the talent of the successors.

59

Mentoring the process, the ultimate legacy.

Successor generations will be able to make decisions based on the best interest of the family, if they hold to the vision, values and process you established. Your mentorship can guide them to develop strategies for meeting any situation now or in the future.

60

Family history, the ultimate role model.

Families who have kept their family and their wealth through multiple generations understand their role and purpose in society through their family history. Each succeeding generation mentors the next to continue the family legacy's contribution to society and their role and purpose in life.

Establish a Method of Family Communication

61

Establish a method of family communication.

How does your family communicate with one another? Is it top down, bottom up, or horizontal? Families that stay together through multiple generations have a method of open intrafamily communication which builds intergenerational relationships.

62

Teach children your decision making process.

How do you make decisions? Are they based on personal values, life experiences, training, or intuition? By sharing your decision making process, you mentor your children in how to make the best decision in any given situation.

63

Teach children the consequences of decisions.

Children learn from their mistakes the same as adults do. There are good and bad choices, each with its own set of outcomes and unintended consequences. Personal accountability for decisions builds self esteem and the self confidence to take responsibility for one's own actions.

64

Communication starts by addressing basic issues.

Mutual respect is necessary for effective communication. Personal boundaries must be honored. Once a person feels safe in sharing his or her views, the family can move to weightier issues. This process allows families to move forward rather than to be snared in old family baggage.

65

Seek to understand your children's perspective.

An old adage suggests perception is reality regardless of whether or not that perception is based on facts. We see, hear, and understand information through our own set of filters. Seeking to understand your children's perspective prevents misunderstanding and breaks down communication barriers.

66

Communicate well so people can't misunderstand.

It seems most of our interpersonal relationship problems stem from seeing and hearing through our own prejudices. If you want a lasting relationship with your children and your in-laws, communicate, speak and listen well, so people can't misunderstand.

67

You always speak as the parent.

You always speak as the parent, and your words are received as one of authority. Adult children need to be able to speak to you as one adult to another. This is a foundation of healthy family relationships.

68

In-laws affect family relationships. Welcome them.

By the time your children marry, your family has been together for two or three decades. How do you welcome the new member to your inner circle? Recognize as a family what you appreciate about that person. It will be beneficial to all.

69

It is their world, not yours.

Conflict in family communication often comes from a clash in generational perspective. Your world is not their world and vice versa. Seek to appreciate your differences rather than letting them escalate into an impenetrable wall that divides the family.

70

Be present in all your communication.

People know when you aren't listening to them. Commit to being present in all your communication. Being present demonstrates respect for others.

Your Heritage Statement Provides Intergenerational Direction

71

The heritage statement: the intergenerational blueprint.

The purpose of a heritage statement is to pass your story to future generations. It clarifies your values, provides your definition of true wealth and conveys your deepest desire for the family's future. It is the guide to implement your sustainable legacy.

72

Memorialize your story for every generation.

The heritage statement is the glue that bonds future generations together. It is the story of the family from its inception. It is the founding document that guides future generations to continue the values and traditions of the family.

73

The heritage statement must reflect you.

The heritage statement must be you in every sense of the word. It must include your phraseology, your attitudes and project your values. It is your voice to inspire and mentor future generations.

74

Prepare to share for maximum impact.

Preparation is essential before sharing your heritage statement with family. Choose a suitable time and place. Advise the family what to expect. A trained, non-family moderator can be valuable in assisting you to deliver a validating experience for all participants.

75

Share the statement. Inspire the family.

Sharing the heritage statement can be an impactful experience because the family gains new insight and appreciation for the parents based on stories they may have never heard. It can unify families and be the catalysis to pursue common family goals.

76

Reveal how you accumulated your wealth.

Future generations will forget how the family wealth was acquired unless you communicate how it was created. Statements like, "Hard work, sweat and tears" do not convey the message. Descibe the specific work, obstacle, success, and failures that made you successful.

77

Establish an order of financial objectives.

Is money a tool to capture opportunities, to provide for education and/or to provide for charitable causes that ignite your passions? In the alternative, is money a means to self-gratification and indulgence? Your view and that of your heirs may differ. The heritage statement can provide financial direction to future generations.

78

Heirs create their vision from you.

The heritage statement presents the parents' vision for their children. Provided you have established the process, the children can expand the family vision to accomplish new goals and to create a new vision for their generation based on family core values.

79

Wealth defined and clarified by vision.

The Rothschilds require every family member to gather annually to review the family history and to reaffirm the mission and values of the family. They believe this is an essential element in keeping the family and the wealth together through generations. They embody the success you should strive for.

80

Create your intergenerational family love letter.

The heritage statement is written to those you care about, sharing what you want most for them. In additon to sharing your history and vision for the future, it is also a love letter to your family illustrating the virtues you hold dear.

Philanthropy Defines Your Values in Life

81

Charitable giving reaffirms your personal blessings.

Every time you give your time and financial wealth to a charitable cause it is a reaffirmation of the blessings in your own life. You could not give if you had not been blessed. Rejoice in your ability to give.

82

Charitable giving is a mentoring tool.

Philanthropy is a process for expressing core values and is an expression of care for others outside of one's immediate family.

83

Family philanthropy provides children financial education.

Involving children in philanthropy gives them the opportunity to manage the process of giving away money. It involves a decision making process which necessitates choosing and comunicating with advisors as well as gaining knowledge of investments, taxes, and budgeting. It provides the opportunity to appreciate money.

84

Philanthropy inspires your legacy for eternity.

Philanthropy has the potential to inspire a personal legacy and allow us to leave a lasting mark. In his book, *The Age of Paradox*, Charles Handy states, "It is a search for a cause. The cause, however, to be truly satisfying must be a 'purpose beyond oneself'."

85

Philanthropy instills a responsibility for wealth.

"The more money you have personally, the more responsiblilty you have to society. Providing an inheritance to our children also gives them certain responsibilities as well, including using their wealth to have a positive impact on society," according to Bob Stone, author and speaker.

86

Philanthropy can minimize the entitlement syndrome.

A friend built houses for people living in a garbage dump. He said he had more wealth on his body than anyone there would have in their lifetime. The next year he took his children along to share the experience. Exposing children to the less fortunate gives them a perspective for the blessings they have received.

87

Define your purpose through your philanthropy.

It doesn't matter what cause you choose to support, but it should match your core values and be larger than yourself. When the cause reflects your values, it excites passion and defines a sense of purpose in your life.

88

Doing good is a family tradition.

Philanthropic dynasties come from family traditions of giving. Children give because their families have taught them it is important to give and they have a high internal motivation to do so. They give because they believe it is everybody's responsibility to do so.

89

Success to significance, paved by philanthropy.

Ask yourself, "How do I wish to be remembered?" "Will my life have made a difference?" Famous people are measured by their accomplishments. Great people are known by their philanthropy.

90

Charities need to know your "Why."

Just as your children need to know why you give, the causes you support need to know why you support them. A philanthropic gift is very personal. It is a reflection of a meaningful experience or a core value. Sharing your "why" can be as impactful to the charity as it is with your family.

Today's Excuse, Tomorrow's Regret. Start Now.

91

Opportunity's window is not open forever.

There are a million excuses and rationalizations that prevent you from starting the process to build your sustainable legacy. We are only guaranteed today. Children regret they did not take the time to learn their parents' stories and parents regret they never shared them.

92

Regret and fear are not excuses.

Negative experiences and broken relations from the past can create regret, avoidance, and fear of family gatherings with children and in-laws. Relationships can be healed, and families reunited. The rewards outweigh the fear and the effort. Start today.

93

Past performance doesn't indicate future results.

When a family can openly communicate without fear; where each member is recognized for their individual value; where the past is forgotten and the focus is on the future, children, long estranged, are often reunited with the family as a result of the legacy process.

94

Will they talk after you're gone?

Family gatherings can be a source of joy and celebration. Unfortunately, they can be marked by heated debate and ill will too. Will your children talk when you're gone? The answer to the question is dependent upon whether or not you establish a process to communicate as a family regarding family business.

95

Avoiding family issues doesn't eliminate them.

All families have issues they avoid addressing. They let them simmer, hoping the lid never comes off the pot. Establish a communication process to enable the family to address conflict in a safe environment. They will have better relationships now and in the future as a result.

96

Dismantle walls by recognizing the positive.

Differences of opinion and ideology can create a sense of ill will. This is especially harmful in family relationships. Even in the worst relationship there is something you can appreciate about another person. Tell them what you admire most about them and watch the walls fall.

97

Each generation moves from parents' values.

Each generation moves further away from the values of their parents. Just like inherited wealth, the first generation experiences it. The second generation hears about it. The third generation never experiences it or hears of it. Each generation must know the family values. It is up to you to create a process to make that happen.

98

Your family really isn't any different.

People often state their family has great relationships and they communicate openly with each other. Dynamics change with births, deaths, marriages and divorces. The family tree expands with grandchildren and cousins. Without a process for the family to communicate, values and wealth are often lost to changing family dynamics.

99

Knowing where
to start is easy.

Your plan starts with your desire to create a sustainable legacy for your family. Next, you develop a process that allows the family to work together to achieve family goals. Often this takes the involvement of a trained professional advisor.

100

Real change requires showing up differently.

What will make your next family gathering different from all those that preceded it? One way is to get the family to think forward rather than backward. Past experiences are forgotten, new relationships and memories are forged by creating positive experiences that unite the family.

Works Cited

Introduction

1. Ming Dynasty quote:
    http://en.wikiquote.org/wiki/Chinese_proverbs;
    The Economist, June 14, 2001, "To have and to
    hold"

2. Holy Bible, I Kings 12

3. Rodney C. Zeeb & Ryan Zeeb, "Guidelines for
    Effective Family Governance," (Portland, Oregon:
    The Heritage Institute, 2009)

4. E.G. "Jay" Link & Peter Tedstrom, "Getting to the
    Heart of the Matter," (Franklin, Indiana:
    Professional Mentoring Program, 1999)

5. Adam Smith, "The Wealth of Nations," (BN
    Publishing, 2009)

Define Your Values. Build Upon Them.

1. Rodney C. Zeeb & Ryan Zeeb, "Guidelines for
    Effective Family Governance," (Portland, Oregon:
    The Heritage Institute, 2009)

Define Success. What's Important to You.

1.   Perry L. Cochell, Rodney C. Zeeb, with Tom Fowler, "Beating the Midas Curse," (Portland, Oregon: Bridgetown Press, 2005)

Shirtsleeves to Shirtsleeves in Three Generations.

1.   Ming Dynasty quote: http://en.wikiquote.org/wiki/Chinese_proverbs, The Economist, June 14, 2001, "To have and to hold"

2.   70% of Estate Planning Fails: Roy Williams & Vic Preisser, "Preparing Hearts, Five Steps to a Successful Transition of Family Wealth and Values," (San Francisco, California: Robert D Reed, 2003)

3.   E.G. "Jay" Link & Peter Tedstrom, "Getting to the Heart of the Matter," (Franklin, Indiana: Professional Mentoring Program, 1999)

4.   Rothschild Family: http://en.wikipedia.org.wiki/Rothschild_family, http://lcf-rothschild.com/en/groue/rothschild/concordia.asp

5.   Holy Bible, Ecclesiastes 2:18-21 (English Standard Version)

6.   Vanderbilt Family:
      http://en.wikipedia.org.wiki/Cornelius_Vanderbil
      t, Arthur T. Vanderbilt 2d, "The Fall of the House
      of Vanderbilt," (New York: William Morrow &
      Company, 1989)

7.   Warren Buffett quote:
      www.brainyquote.com/quotes/authors/w/warren
      _buffett.html, USA Today, July 26, 2006, "Should
      kids be left fortunes, or be left out?"

8   Vanderbilt Family:
      http://en.wikipedia.org.wiki/Cornelius_Vanderbil
      t, Arthur T. Vanderbilt 2d, "The Fall of the House
      of Vanderbilt," (New York: William Morrow &
      Company, 1989)

9.   Affluenza: Jessie H. O'Neill, "The Golden Ghetto"
      (Milwaukee, Wisconsin: The Affluenza Project,
      1997)

Understanding Family Roles Create Lasting Legacies

1.   Ernest A. Doud, Jr. & Lee Hausner, Ph.D., "Hats
      Off to You" (2000)

2.   Thomas E. Fowler, CLU, "The Impact of Family
      Dynamics on Succession Planning," (NAIFA
      Financial Forum, Dallas, Texas, 2008)

3.   Ernest A. Doud, Jr. & Lee Hausner, Ph.D., "Hats Off to You" (2000)

4.   Thomas E. Fowler, CLU, "The Impact of Family Dynamics on Succession Planning," (NAIFA Financial Forum, Dallas, Texas, 2008)

5.   Ernest A. Doud, Jr. & Lee Hausner, Ph.D., "Hats Off to You" (2000)

6.   Jeffrey Sonnefeld, "The Hero's Farewell: What Happens When CEOs Retire," (New York, NY: Oxford University Press, Inc, 1988)

7.   Ernest A. Doud, Jr. & Lee Hausner, Ph.D., "Hats Off to You" (2000)

8.   Rodney C. Zeeb & Ryan Zeeb, "Guidelines for Effective Family Governance," (Portland, Oregon: The Heritage Institute, 2009)

Establish a Method of Family Communication
1.   Thomas E. Fowler, CLU, "The Impact of Family Dynamics on Succession Planning," (NAIFA Financial Forum, Dallas, Texas, 2008)

Your Heritage Statement Provides Intergenerational Direction.

1   Rodney C. Zeeb & Ryan Zeeb, "Guidelines for Effective Family Governance," (Portland, Oregon: The Heritage Institute, 2009)

Philanthropy Defines Your Values in Life

1.   Collier, Chares W., "Wealth in Families" (2003)

2.   Prince, Russ Alan & File, Karen Maru, "The Seven Faces of Philanthropy," (1994)

3.   Handy, Charles, "The Age of Paradox," (Harvard Business School Press, Boston, MA, 1994)

Today's Excuse, Tomorrow's Regret. Start Now

1.   Holy Bible, Proverbs 22:6

I hope this book has been helpful to you and that you are able to take a few nuggets and put them into action to secure your own lasting family legacy. To engage me to guide your family to create a sustainable family legacy contact me at:

The Fowler Group

Thomas E. Fowler

President

Phone: 800-999-5300 x23 * 425-453-1585 x23

Email: tom@fowlerfinanical.com

fowlerfinancial.com

Keynotes & Seminars with Tom Fowler

Tom Fowler is the president of The Fowler Group and he has authored numerous articles regarding business and estate planning issues for closely held and family owned businesses. Tom has worked with a number of families to assist them in creating sustainable family legacies. He was a contributing author for the book, *Beating the Midas Curse*, a publication of The Heritage Institute.

Tom Fowler is a thought provoking and sought after speaker. His wisdom and insights on family legacy planning, leadership, business transition planning inspire action and earn rave reviews.

Tom's speaking and writing engagements have included:

- *The Impact of Family Dynamics on Succession Planning*, Washington State Bar Association
- *The Exit Planning Solution*, Family Office Planning & Management Forum, Florida
- *How to Maximize Relationships through the Heritage Process,* National Association of Insurance Financial Advisors
- *Family Legacy Planning,* Children's Hospital Donors Society
- *The Question of Succession*, Advance Leadership Forum, INLD, Toral, Spain

- *How to Structure a Family Business Succession Plan to Give More to the Family & Less to the IRS,* Estate Planning Council, Texas
- *The Third Element of Estate Planning,* Benefactor's Society Sponsored by the Overlake Hospital Foundation
- *The Power of the Interesting Questions,* The Heritage Institute
- *Listening Between the Lines Opens Opportunities,* Million Dollar Roundtable Magazine

To book Tom Fowler for your next conference or in-house event, please contact:

Thomas E. Fowler
The Fowler Group
800-999-5300 (x23)
tom@fowlerfinancial.com
fowlerfinancial.com

See the entire Six-Word Lesson Series at
6wordlessons.com

7784107R0

Made in the USA
Charleston, SC
09 April 2011